Composting Abbie:
A Whale of a Story

Composting Abbie:
A Whale of a Story

by Jed Diamond
Illustrated by Ann Meyer Maglinte

Fifth Wave Press • Willits, California

Composting Abbie: A Whale of a Story
Text Copyright © 2014 by Jed Diamond
Published by Fifth Wave Press
Box 442, Willits, California 95490

Illustrations copyright © 2014 by Ann Meyer Maglinte
The full-color artwork was prepared with watercolors on Arches watercolor paper
Photographic references by Larry Wagner and Ron LeValley, both of Fort Bragg, California

Layout and edits by Jerri-Jo Idarius of Willits, California; www.Creation-Designs.com

Library of Congress Cataloging-in-Publication Data
Diamond, Jed
Composting Abbie: A Whale of a Story

Paperback: ISBN-13:978-0-911761-02-3 and ISBN-10:0911761020
Hardback: ISBN-13:978-0-911761-05-4 and ISBN-10:0911761055
Ebook: ISBN-13:978-0-911761-04-7 and ISBN-10:0911761047

Children's age range 9-12 to adult
Animals
Nature
Conservation
Recycling

Acknowledgements and Appreciations

I'd like to thank the following people who made this book and the telling of this story possible. Ann Meyer Maglinte visited Cold Creek Compost, heard the story and painted the wonderful pictures that illustrate the book. Martin Mileck is a visionary and story teller. He had the brilliant idea of composting the whale and turning her into flowers and food for the children. Jerri-Jo Idarius did the layout and design work for the book. Many people in the community helped with this project.

Abbie Colbert and Tom Mitchell deserve credit for giving Martin the chance to prove that a whale can be successfully composted. Abbie felt there was a better way to deal with a dead whale and made the call to Cold Creek Compost. Tom Mitchell, former CEO of Mendocino County, had faith in Martin and directed regulatory agencies to allow the whale to be composted. Martin also wants to thank to Jeff Archer who volunteered to haul the whale and all the other people who donated their time and equipment.

Hi my name is Stuart, Stu for short. I have lived in Fort Bragg all my life. I'm a seagull, and my best friend has been a blue whale named Abbie. We grew up together, and what great adventures we had! We explored every part of the Mendocino coast and saw things that most humans will never see.

I was so proud of Abbie when she birthed a beautiful calf. I loved to fly overhead while both of them were swimming.

Did you know that blue whales are the largest animal living on our earth? They are even bigger than the biggest dinosaur. The story of what happened to my friend, Abbie, is an amazing tale. I saw it all. Seagulls don't miss much. You may not believe what I'm going to tell you, but it's absolutely true—every word of it.

One day the three of us went out to our favorite ocean spot. It was a beautiful day. Abbie and her calf were having a great time playing tag and did not notice the ship coming their way. The people on the ship did not see them either. That's pretty amazing since Abbie was over seventy feet long. That's about the length of three school buses. Her baby was over twenty-five feet long, about the size of two mini-vans.

Abbie's ancestors have been swimming the waters of our world for fifty million years, but now they are an endangered species. They used to be hunted for their oil, blubber and meat, but now they are protected by law. However, they aren't protected from the many ships they share the sea with.

I tried to warn Abbie about the ship, but it was too late.

The newspapers reported the tragedy.

On the Mendocino Coast south of Fort Bragg Monday evening, a large blue whale was struck by a research vessel. The whale body is in an inlet just south of the word-famous Mendocino Coast Botanical Gardens.

But I knew what had happened. I had seen it and could not stop my tears. I had lost my best friend. Many people from the community came down to the beach to see Abbie. Students from Humboldt State University's Marine Program in Arcata even came to see and evaluate the whale.

You can see in the picture how big the whale is compared the size of the humans who came to learn what they could about his magnificent creature.

More people came. It seemed that everyone was interested in Abbie, even though she was no longer alive. There was a big gash on her side where she was hit by the boat.

A reporter from National Geographic News wrote a report and took pictures.

These whales are rare and it's even rarer to see one that has so recently died.

Abbie provided the researchers with a wonderful opportunity to learn.

Humboldt State University mammal expert, Thor Holmes, said,

I'm as sorry as anybody that the animal perished, but to find a fresh, female blue whale in a place that's accessible so we can study her— that is amazing.

While the reporters, scientists, teachers and students were excited to be learning about the whale, there was one big problem. No one knew what to do with the whale body, and it was starting to smell.

It was one thing to study a huge mammal weighing seventy tons. It was another thing to figure out what to do after people stopped looking at it.

Laura, a local resident, had heard of a man named Martin who lived further inland and composts all sorts of things like spoiled food, lawn clippings, brush and even manure. She called him up. *We've got a whale of a problem here and we need your help.*

Martin responded, *We take almost anything, even things that smell really bad, but we've never tried to compost a whole whale. Let me think about it, and I'll get back to you right away.*

Martin owns Cold Creek Compost and has been making compost for a long time. Here he is in front of a large pile of compost.

He had a brilliant idea. It was as if a light bulb had turned on in his head. *I know I can compost this whale instead of sending her to a dump site.*

Compost is the best and most complete fertilizer. You can grow anything with compost. It provides all the essential nutrients and micro-organisms essential to soil health.

We'll give the whale compost to schools and community gardens, Martin thought.

He called Laura right back and told her he could do it. All they had to do was load the whale blubber onto trucks and move it to his facility. Then he would turn it into compost that could be used to grow food for many families.

With the good news from Martin, Laura sprang into action. She had her own brilliant idea. *What if we could take out the bones and reassemble them later into a skeleton of a blue whale? What an educational resource it would be for adults and kids.*

She called her friends and neighbors and put out the word to the community. The next thing I knew, the beach was full of people! There were close to 200 volunteers, young and old. They were ready to help prepare the whale for composting and salvage a skeleton of the biggest animal that has ever lived on this earth.

I watched as they worked. Now I could see that Abbie would be remembered for years to come. Her skeleton would be on display, and her body would be converted into compost that would help grow food for the community.

This is Jennifer. She's a student at Humboldt State University. She and the other students came to see the whale and to help.

It was a bigger job than they expected and the smell was really bad. The weather was cold and damp. This was some of the hardest work she had ever done—even after the whale's bones were removed.

How do you get fifty tons of whale up to the top of a steep hill? She learned that you do it one ton at a time. One ton is really heavy. It is the equivalent of 2,000 pounds.

First, the students had to cut the whale into pieces. The Roach brothers helped out by using their logging equipment to haul the whale up the hill to the trucks. The skeleton would be cleaned and assembled later for display, and the blubber would be trucked to Martin for composting.

This was a big day—the last day needed to haul the last of the whale blubber up the hill.

The people were really tired after cutting one ton chunks of whale and tying chains around each piece. The tractor pulled the sections up the forty-foot cliff, high above the beach.

Have you ever tried to drag a one-ton load of whale up a steep cliff? I'll tell you, it doesn't look easy, but with a lot of help and cooperation, the job was completed.

I was glad that something wonderful was going to come out of this very sad event.

Like everything else about a blue whale, the bones are huge. There are only five complete blue whale skeletons in the whole country. The researchers wanted to learn everything they could about the bones.

The bones had to be measured and then loaded on to the big trucks.

I can't imagine anything more exciting than this, said Laura. *The bones will be taken to a secret, magical resting place in the woods where they will be buried for two years. The micro-organisms in the soil will eat away all the flesh and clean them before they are put back together. Then everyone can study and enjoy Abbie's full skeleton.*

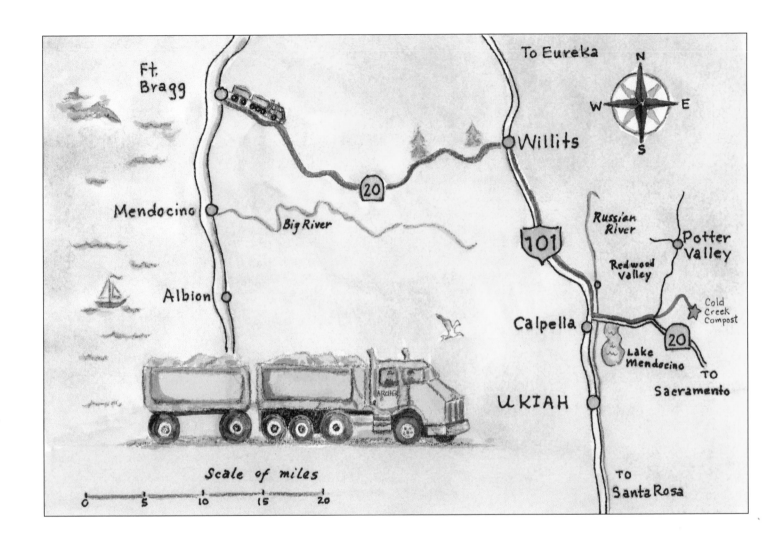

Here's a map of where it all happened. Abbie, the whale, was hit in the ocean and washed ashore in Fort Bragg, California. The whale had to be hauled fifty miles to Cold Creek Compost near Potter Valley.

Fort Bragg is on the coast of Mendocino County, in Northern California. The town has a lot to offer and is a popular place to visit because of its beautiful views of the Pacific Ocean and the rugged Northern California coastline.

The big yellow truck that brought Abbie to the compost facility is proudly owned by Jeff Archer. Look closely and you can see him driving.

I lead the way as they drove inland, because I was excited to see how compost was made and to meet Martin.

Oh my! Here we are at Cold Creek Compost. Have you ever seen a compost facility before?

Cold Creek is a place of constant activity. There are big machines and people at work all day, every day. There are lots of trucks and loaders. Martin's office is on the right hand side with the flowers growing in front.

The pond you see in the foreground is very important. It collects all the run-off water from the composting process so it doesn't go into the creeks. All this water is reused. That way water from the streams is conserved. A good composting facility reuses everything.

In the background you can see the roof that protects the compost from the rain.

When we arrived, Martin was there to welcome us. I liked him right away. You might not think that a composting facility would be a place you'd want to visit, but it is amazing to see how something that might hurt the earth can be turned into something that will help the earth.

I love to give tours, show kids and adults what we do here, and share with them why we do it, says Martin. *We can compost almost anything except glass, metal or plastic. Come for a visit. There's a lot you can learn.*

We take materials that would go into a land fill or pollute the environment and make a wonderful fertilizer that local farmers need in order to grow food.

Here is one of our trucks, bringing in waste that no one else wants. We want it, says Martin. *For us there's no such thing as waste. Everything can and should be recycled.*

The whale pieces have arrived! Soon they will become compost and be on their way to a farm to make the soil rich and ready to grow crops.

Sometimes the compost is delivered to a vineyard where grapes are grown. Other times it goes to a local farm where people grow vegetables.

Some people still spend a lot of money buying fertilizers made from chemicals. Compost is the best fertilizer and costs less than chemical-based fertilizers. It provides all the nutrients that are needed to grow food.

It's nice to know we are re-using and not wasting valuable resources.

What's this interesting machine? It's a grinder.

This is the first step in the composting process. Everything is ground up before composting can begin.

Here, pieces of the whale are being loaded into the grinder where they are ground into little bits. The little pieces of whale will be mixed with other materials such as ground-up yard trimmings and wood waste. When they are all mixed together, they will make really good compost.

You might think it is easy to cut up pieces of whale blubber, but it is actually quite difficult. Because, whale meat is really tough, the grinder had to work very hard to do the whole job. After it was accomplished, we were ready for the next step . . . .

Wow! This process is hard to see.

There is a driver on the top of this big machine. It is called a compost turner and is turning a 'windrow' of compost. A windrow is just a long pile of compost.

You can hardly see the machine because of all the steam. The micro-organisms in the compost create lots of heat. Just like humans, they need oxygen and the compost turner makes sure there is enough air coming in. Material on the inside comes to the outside and material that was on the outside gets into the middle. The material gets so hot, steam can be seen rising from the windrows.

That's important because if there isn't enough air, the wrong organisms grow and things start to smell. Waste products come in here smelling really bad, but when the process is finished, the compost smells great.

This is also the compost turner.

Here, it is blending a batch of potting soil. It mixes things like wood ash, rice hulls, lava rock, and wood waste all together. These ingredients create a perfect mixture for growing things. You can use potting soil to fill pots or raised beds so that home gardeners can grow flowers and food.

This is the compost screen. I like its bright colors.

Screening is the final step in the production of compost.

It screens out the bigger pieces of material that have not decomposed completely to become compost. These are sent back to the grinder so they can finish decomposing. Nothing is wasted.

Other facilities send this kind of material away to be burned or buried in a landfill but, at Cold Creek Compost, it is recycled.

The finished product is sold to customers such as local vineyards who grow grapes and to vegetable farmers who grow a lot of the food we eat.

This is the day we have been waiting for!

Here is Jeff Archer in his truck delivering the finished compost to people all around the area.

Martin decided to give away the special Abbie-the-Whale compost to many schools, churches and community organizations, including Blosser Lane Elementary School, Nokomis School, Grace Lutheran Church, the Boys and Girls Club, Howard Memorial Hospital Community Garden, Lake County Tribal Health, Plowshares and Mendocino College.

It was a big event when the truck arrived at this school. The children and I were so excited, because we knew this compost would help grow the best food and flowers.

The children love to play while they work. By letting them get their hands dirty and have lots of fun, they enjoy growing their own food. When they have grown their own carrots, lettuce, and tomatoes, they will want to eat carrots, lettuce, and tomatoes. That also makes parents happy, as they want their children to eat healthy food.

It was a cold morning at the school, but the kids loved spreading the healthy compost in the vegetable garden.

Knowing Abbie helped make this happen, makes me happy.

We know that a lot of our waste goes into garbage dumps. If you've ever seen one, you know you don't want to spend a lot of time there.

The garbage dump smells bad and looks bad. From bicycle tires to television sets, you will find so many things there. You would be amazed to know how much of the stuff that ends up in a dump can be turned into compost.

If we learned to recycle and reuse what we have, we wouldn't have so much waste. At Cold Creek Compost, Martin uses food scraps, soiled paper, wood, lawn clippings, branches, sheet rock, asphalt shingles and much more to make compost. His goal is to eliminate waste.

We should recycle everything we can to keep our earth healthy.

This is what happens to our beautiful mountains when we don't compost. The top picture shows an open pit mine. Here, the land is torn up in order to extract the minerals that lie buried deep in the earth. The mountains are destroyed. When they are gone, there is nowhere for the animals to live. By recycling what we have, instead of burying it in landfills, we can reduce this destruction.

The picture below shows an incineration plant burning waste that could be composted. People burn waste because they think it is easier than composting, but burning unwanted materials is short-sighted and pollutes the air. My bird brothers and sisters get sick and die. What seemed easy, turns out to be a big problem and affects people's health too. Martin has a better way.

Composting can help save our world!

My friends and I love to visit the land near the Cold Creek Compost facility. It is on the Guntly Ranch.

The valley in this picture is also part of the Ranch. It was going to be turned into a landfill for garbage. Martin and Cold Creek Compost helped to keep that from happening.

By composting all the material that was going into the landfill, instead of a valley of garbage, now there is a beautiful place and lots of good, rich compost.

Humans don't have to create more and more waste and garbage. Instead they can support a healthy cycle of life for the animals, the children, and for future generations.

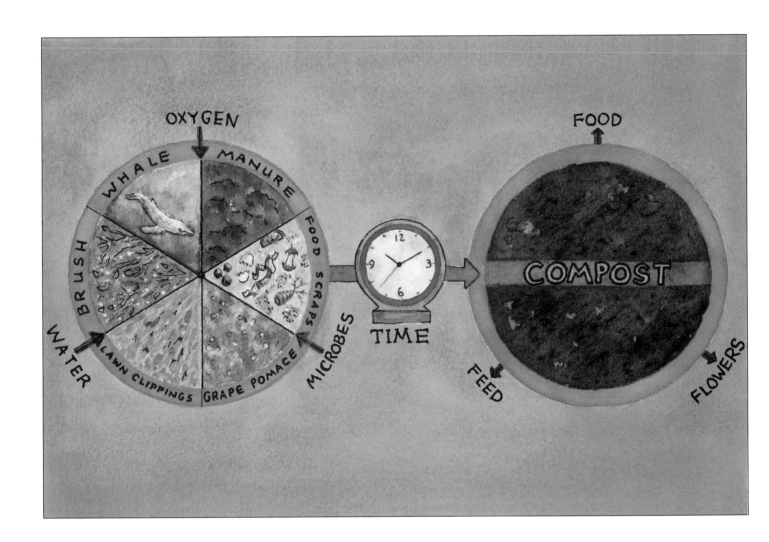

This is a simple way of telling the whole story about what happened to Abbie.

Believe me, if you can compost the largest mammal on earth, you can compost anything. At Cold Creek Compost, Martin mixed whale parts with manure, food scraps, grape skins, lawn clippings, and brush. Air and water were added and then millions of tiny creatures called micro-organisms digested everything. All it took was a little time for those micro-organisms to transform the yucky stuff into dark, rich, pleasant smelling compost that was used to grow flowers and food for people and animals.

In the end, there was no waste . . . only food and flowers.

I miss Abbie a lot, but I like to imagine her swimming happily in a beautiful place not on this earth. Whenever you go to the ocean, you can think of Abbie. Her whale spirit lives on in the compost she helped create and in our awareness of how we can help the earth. Whenever you're in your garden, her spirit will be with you.

If you want to have an up-close-and-personal experience of Abbie's story come to Mendocino County and trace Abbie's route from the ocean's edge in Fort Bragg to the Cold Creek Compost facility near Potter Valley.

Ask for Martin. He will be happy to show you around and tell you the whole story. Maybe you will even see me there. Look up, wave, and say, *Hi, Stuart.*

The story of life goes on and on. Abbie's baby is now a grown whale and has her own life in the sea. We play together, just like her mom and I did. I hope we will have many adventures.

It is true, we are all part of the web of life. Birds, the ocean, plants, animals and people are all connected. If we take care of the earth, the earth and all its creatures will be here for many generations to come.

There is no end to this story.

Martin Mileck and Cold Creek Compost

Martin grew up during the nineteen sixties on the campus of U.C. Berkeley, where he learned to think independently and question convention. In the early eighties he went on to open a farm supply/hardware store in Covelo, California and teach himself to farm.

Martin sees value in what others throw away. As a farmer, Martin realized that what we, as a society, bury in landfills can be used by farmers to grow crops. Using compost also allows people to farm more profitably and with less environmental impact than using traditional chemicals. In 1995 Martin opened Cold Creek Compost and continued a career of helping farmers improve their operations while at the same time bringing much needed change to the garbage industry.

Cold Creek Compost is the first permitted compost facility in the North Coast Region, an area that includes Santa Rosa and stretches to the Oregon border. Cold Creek has the highest level of permitting possible and composts a wide variety of materials including manures, dead chickens, wood, food waste, cat litter, fish guts, brewery waste, power plant ash, and much more. All of these materials are made of valuable plant nutrients that would go to waste if buried in landfills.

The Cold Creek Compost facility was very carefully sited in the middle of the 2700 acre Guntly Ranch. This assures minimal impact to neighbors from noise, dust or odors associated with the composting process. Built to exceptionally high standards, the facility assures the least possible environmental impact.

Since its inception, Cold Creek has been the largest recycler in a multi-county area. Cold Creek is able to recycle fully half of the municipal waste stream, making it the paradigm of the future for recycling rather than burying or burning our resources.

Cold Creek Compost Inc.
6000 Potter Valley Road
Ukiah, Ca, 95428
707-485-5966
coldcreekcompost.com

Author, Jed Diamond

Jed Diamond has a passionate interest in life and how people can learn to live in balance with nature, with themselves, with other people, and with all the other creatures of the earth. He is most well-known for his work in the field of gender medicine and men's health. This is his first book for children and adults who can still see the world through the eyes of a child.

Diamond has been a licensed psychotherapist for more than forty years. He has a master's degree in social work and a PhD in International Health.

He lives with his wife, Carlin, on Shimmins Ridge, above Bloody Run Creek, in Northern California. They are proud parents of five grown children and fifteen grandchildren.

To stay in touch: website: MenAlive.com, email: Jed@MenAlive.com, phone: (707) 459-5505, mailing address: Box 442, Willits, California 95490

Watercolor Illustrations, Ann Meyer Maglinte

Ann Meyer Maglinte has always loved watercolors since she was given her first set of Prang pan watercolors as a child and began drawing animals for imaginary children's books. Several years later her uncle gave her an antique dip pen set, and so began her love of pen and ink and calligraphy.

She graduated with a Bachelor of Arts degree from San Jose State University and has since worked as a graphic designer, craftsperson, herbalist, teacher, musician and caterer. In the 1980s Ann was commissioned to do pen and ink illustrations and maps for several books by Teresa Edgerton, including The Green Lion Trilogy—all published by Ace/Berkley Publishing Group.

Ann has taught watercolor for many years at Mendocino College and continues to teach, do graphic design and book illustration. Her paintings are in collections all over the world. Ann also sculpts the garden plaques for Midnight Moon Designs, the business she and her husband, Jon, own. Their work can be seen at Northcoast Artists Gallery in Fort Bragg, near Mendocino.

Ann and her family live in a rambling house in the countryside of Willits, California, with their 3 cats, 2 dogs and a hamster. She has always loved the sea, and was very inspired by the tale of Abbie the Whale. She feels, as many do, that the time is now to re-use, recycle, compost and take care of our mother earth. To see more about Ann and her art: www.annmaglinte.com